C000240725

The Georgian Household

by
Jean Ellenby
illustrated by
Juliet Stanwell-Smith

Produced by Dinosaur Publications for
Cambridge University Press

Cambridge
London   New York   New Rochelle
Melbourne   Sydney

The Georgian age

The Four Georges, George I, George II, George III and George IV gave their name to an age of increasing wealth and great elegance in Britain – the Georgian period.

When, in 1714, George I arrived from Hanover to be crowned King of England, Abraham Darby had already discovered that iron could be smelted using coke for fuel instead of wood, which was becoming scarce; farmers had begun to improve their methods of stock breeding and crop rotation; and heavily laden merchant ships were sailing across the world's oceans to trade with exotic countries. As this growth in trade and knowledge was developing, landowners, merchants and industrialists began to grow richer. There were huge profits to be made in farming, commerce and manufacture and as fortunes grew, so the standard of living rose.

The Georgian period was an age of beautiful country houses, built in a style and taste which reflected the wealth of their owners. Rich men employed the finest architects, designers and landscape gardeners to create magnificent estates. They collected statues, ornaments and art treasures, had huge portraits painted to decorate the spacious interiors, and ordered furniture in the latest styles from cabinet makers who became world famous.

Although most wealthy families worked hard they also knew how to enjoy themselves and a good deal of time was spent hunting, shooting and fishing or playing cricket or quoits on the lawn. After dinner, which was an enormous meal of meats, pies and fruit, card games or dice were played by candlelight. Sometimes a musical evening would be arranged – perhaps around the newly invented pianoforte. But the biggest treat of the year was 'The Season'. During the winter, whole families travelled to London in horse-drawn carriages for a hectic round of theatre visits, glittering balls and brilliant parties, before returning to their splendid houses in the country to organize the activity of the estate for another year.

Changes in farming

When most people in Britain lived in the country, they only needed enough land to grow food for themselves. The open fields round the village were divided into lots of narrow strips which were shared more or less equally between the peasants. To avoid arguments about the richness or stoniness of the soil, the strips cultivated by each family were scattered in different parts of the estate.

During the Industrial Revolution, thousands of people moved into the newly built towns, seeking work in the factories. They no longer had the land, or the time, to grow their own food, and farmers found the new townspeople a growing market for their vegetables, meat and grain. But it was exhausting and difficult trying to grow food efficiently in tiny strips. Since before Tudor times some landowners had been turning the peasants off the land in order to enclose it. With the Enclosure Acts, Parliament made this practice legal, and during the eighteenth century there was a rapid increase in the number of peasants forced to give their land to the landlord, who compensated them with a few coins or perhaps a small plot on the edge of the village. Energetic landowners divided the land into fields by planting hedges and tried new methods of farming. They were often successful and grew extremely rich.

One of the biggest problems in farming was how to feed the cattle and sheep during the long winter months when grass stops growing. Charles Townshend, the second viscount, was a Member of Parliament, but after a fierce quarrel with the Prime Minister he resigned

his seat and returned to his estate in Norfolk. There, to the amusement of his friends, he began to grow lots of turnips in all his fallow fields. In derision they nicknamed him 'Turnip Townshend'. But he showed that root crops could be fed to animals all winter, making the mass autumn slaughter of cattle to be salted for storage unnecessary. In this way, fresh meat could be provided all the year round. What is more, the animals, while munching their way through the turnip fields, were richly manuring the land for the later sowing of corn!

Now that fields were being enclosed and animals were prevented from wandering freely over the common land, farmers began to control the breeding of their stock. Because wool was such an important industry in Britain, a good sheep had always been judged by the length and fluffiness of its fleece. Robert Bakewell decided that sheep with lower quality wool could be bred for their mutton. He produced a fine strain of Leicestershire sheep which helped to increase the supply of meat for the nation, and made his fortune by hiring out the rams to other farmers for breeding. Soon, more and more farmers followed Bakewell's lead in selectively breeding animals, either for their meat or for their wool. People were so interested in the size of these new breeds that many artists painted pictures showing huge square beasts of exaggerated size, dwarfing the men admiring them.

Farmers throughout the country were benefitting from the improvements in agriculture. By adopting the new methods and experimenting on their own, the quantity and quality of the crops they produced increased enormously and it was only by these advances that the growing populations in the towns could be fed.

Building

Many landowners had become very wealthy because of improvements in agriculture and the increase in overseas trade. They spent vast fortunes employing well-known architects, builders and craftsmen to build splendid houses on their country estates.

Because so many people were travelling round the Continent, interest in foreign architecture increased, particularly in the work of an Italian called Andrea Palladio. He had carefully studied classical Roman architecture, calculating how the elegant proportions were attained and sketching the slender columns and delicate mouldings. During the sixteenth century he used this knowledge to build many graceful country villas near Vicenza for noblemen. These were admired and imitated by British architects in the Georgian period and this style became known as 'Palladian'. Lord Burlington was so impressed by Palladio's work that he arranged for several young men to study architecture in Italy. Robert Adam, the great Scottish architect, developed a lighter touch, filling his buildings with charm and delicacy. The rooms he designed often had semi-circular walls and the distinctive plaster decorations for which he became famous.

Houses were usually symmetrical on the outside, with imposing pillared entrances. Two wings, identical in design, were often attached to the central block – one would contain the kitchen and servants' quarters, the other housed horses and grooms. Sash windows were introduced in the Georgian period and these, too, were symmetrically placed. A very heavy tax on houses with more than seven windows did not seem to make much difference to the number of windows in these grand mansions. Occasionally some false windows would be used, but these were more to preserve the balanced look of the façade than to save tax.

These magnificent houses took years to build; armies of workmen were employed and huge quantities of materials were used. Everything had to be carted to the site by horse and wagon. Timber from the nearby forest or bricks made from local clay meant fairly short journeys, but many goods had to be carried for much longer distances. Stone was considered to be much grander in appearance than brick, and to save costs many houses were built in ordinary brick and then covered with a thin outer layer of stone. This created the desired classical effect. Often this stone could not be obtained locally. One proud owner was apparently so distressed when George III visited his home and remarked in disgust 'Brick!', that he promptly had the entire house faced with Portland stone.

The builders began work while the materials were being brought to the site. Foundations were dug and laid; wooden scaffolding was erected. Brick by brick or stone by stone the structure grew. Stonemasons shaped the blocks, and pillars were carefully sculpted with hammer and chisel. Window frames were constructed and fitted; carpenters cut the timber for the joists and floorboards; and the great roof beams were fixed in place. As the building rose, plasterers and decorators applied their skills to the interior, and finally the scaffolding was removed, the building completed and the glory of the design revealed. So long did the building take that the man who had commissioned it was sometimes dead before it was finished.

Furniture and art

As trade expanded, new woods were brought back from the great tropical forests, but it was only after 1733, when the tax on imported wood was abolished, that mahogany began to be commonly used in this country. At great expense it was brought across the sea from the West Indies in sailing sloops, and wealthy merchants and landowners were soon furnishing their houses with this dark wine-coloured wood. Before this, most furniture had been made from sturdy oak, which was easy to obtain from the local forests, and was very solid and heavy. Sometimes plain beech wood was covered with a thin layer of walnut, called a véneer, which was cut so that the golden swirling grain made a rich pattern across the furniture.

In their grand houses the gentry wanted furniture that would look elegant in the beautifully proportioned rooms. Cabinet makers were consulted and during this period they designed piece after piece of exquisite furniture. Three names are particularly associated with eighteenth-century furniture, but it is extremely unlikely that they designed all the chairs, tables and cabinets that are recognized as 'Chippendale', 'Hepplewhite' or 'Sheraton'. In their workshops they produced fine furniture in distinctive styles and it is certain that these shapes were copied by other craftsmen throughout the country. Each of the master craftsmen published a book of his designs. Chippendale's, which came out in 1754, was called 'The Gentleman and Cabinet Maker's Directory'. Landowners choosing a new chair or bureau would use these as pattern books to show the local cabinet maker what they wanted.

Nearly all the furniture of this period was elaborately carved on the front but left very plain on the back. This was because the furniture was neatly arranged against the walls of a room and there seemed little point in spending hours hand-carving beautiful patterns for nobody to see. At mealtimes occasional tables were used and these were joined together with hinged flaps for special dinners.

The Georgians were enthusiastic collectors of shining glass, elegant silver, and delicate china. These graced the table at their splendid meals. Different sizes of forks and spoons for each course became fashionable. Beautiful silver coffee and tea pots were used for the recently imported hot drinks which had become such a well-established habit. Visitors were always offered a 'dish of tay' because tea was drunk from dishes (cups with no handles). 'Flint' glass had recently been invented. This was far less brittle than the traditional Venetian glass and often had intricate patterns cut into it, making it sparkle like crystal as the light reflected brilliantly from the grooves and angles of the cuts.

Nearly all the country gentry had huge, stern portraits of their families painted, with backgrounds showing views of their estates in the far distance. It was a satisfying way to decorate the long blank walls of the huge rooms and also ensured that future generations could see pictures of their ancestors. For this was long before cameras, recording a scene in a few seconds, were invented. Often the artist stayed at the house while he completed his masterpieces, but very famous portrait painters like Sir Joshua Reynolds or Thomas Gainsborough opened studios in London or Bath where fashionable gentry, actors, musicians and statesmen were eager to sit for the Master. William Hogarth was another portrait painter, who also drew many cartoon-like sketches of life. They are full of horrifying, sad or amusing details as he tried to show just how cruel, vulgar and bored many of his subjects were and the appalling number of social problems that were being ignored in this period.

Young men travelling abroad on the Grand Tour bought enormous landscape paintings and classical statues, which were carefully packed in boxes and sent home by wagon and ship. Months later, when they arrived, the footmen carefully unwrapped them and struggled to place them exactly as the mistress thought they looked best.

A few adventurous travellers went to the Orient and arrived home with crates of exquisite china, rolls of expensive wallpaper and lots of exciting new ideas. Before long every wealthy household had at least one or two pieces of 'Chinese' furniture, actually made by local craftsmen and elaborately carved with bells, temples or delicate lattice work, imitating the curious angular look of genuine imported pieces. Many extravagant men ordered large shipments of original ornaments and furniture, and a 'Chinese room' in the house became almost commonplace. The Prince Regent imported tons of Chinese furnishings for the Royal Pavilion at Brighton, where even the outside of the building reflects the eastern influence and the kitchen ceiling is supported by pillars that look like tall palm trees!

Housekeeping and its problems

Under practically every four-poster bed was a chamber pot, emptied daily by a maid trying hard not to sniff the stinking fumes. A few houses had water closets, which were a tremendous extravagance, and needed very elaborate drainage and water systems. But even these usually became badly clogged and dreadfully smelly.

Sewage was not the only problem of life in a Georgian house. The new canals made it possible for coal to be carried easily across the country. Gradually people began to burn coal in their fireplaces instead of logs from the dwindling forests. But coal produces far more soot than wood does and this tended to block the flue and unexpectedly fall on the fire below. Clouds of black soot tumbling down the chimney would soon ruin the appearance of a classical marble mantelpiece with its carved floral garlands and Greek urns. The answer was to send for a chimney sweep. The sweep would bring a small 'climbing boy' with him who was sent clambering up the shaft with orders to brush it clean. As the space was so narrow, only pathetically thin boys, who had probably been deliberately starved by their masters, could get through. Often they were absolutely terrified of the darkness, the choking dust and the scorching bricks, but if they protested the sweep would force them to climb by pricking the soles of their feet with a pin on the end of a stick and sometimes even by lighting a fire underneath them. Many boys became so ill from the filthy soot and hard work that they died after a few years, and some actually suffocated in the chimneys. Although the Government changed the law to try and protect children from such appalling working conditions, 'climbing boys' were employed to sweep chimneys until the middle of the nineteenth century.

At sunset, when it became difficult to see, a servant was summoned to bring a taper and light the candles in the candlesticks or on the cut-glass chandeliers. In the 1760s bell-pulls were invented which made an enormous difference to the organization of the household. Maids could now work in the kitchen or the servants' quarters, perhaps polishing the splendid silver or the beautiful glass decanters. As soon as a bell rang they could easily see from the bell-board where they were needed, and quickly wiping their hands scurry to answer the call. Before bell systems were installed servants stood outside doors for hours on end, waiting to be asked to run different errands. They often became exceedingly bored, sometimes even falling asleep!

The mistress of an eighteenth-century house had to be a superb organizer. She controlled an army of servants and made sure that the whole household was supplied with all the provisions it needed.

Tall loaves of sugar, exotic spices such as nutmeg, cinnamon or pepper, and sackfuls of dried fruit were all expensive items, but could now be bought from the grocer in the nearest town. Apples, plums, blackberries, strawberries, nectarines, walnuts and hazel nuts, grew in the gardens or wild in the fields. Meat, game and fish were caught or shot on the estate, and meals were planned using foods in season. But there were many things which still had to be made in the house. Soap, candles, ink, bread, butter, cheese and beer were all made at home and each production had to be carefully supervised. Although the housekeeper did much of the work, it was the mistress who had the final responsibility and personally made sure that everything was in order.

Soap-making was a typical chore. Great lumps of animal fat were melted down and mixed with soda. Then a few herbs were tossed in to improve the smell. This ritual took place only occasionally, but others, like cheese-making or brewing beer, happened much more often.

Usually, the sole supply of water was from a hand-pump in the yard. Pailful after pailful had to be lugged into the house for washing and cooking, and jug after jug carried up long flights of stairs to washstands in the bedrooms. An enormous kettle hung over the kitchen fire and this was the only source of hot water for the entire house.

Bathrooms were extremely rare. If the master wanted a bath, he climbed into a tin one placed in front of the fire in his room. The difficulties with the water supply and the fact that so many clothes were made of brocade or velvet, which were totally ruined by washing, meant that people were often very grimy and smelly. It seems that one fine lady was not at all embarrassed when someone commented on her filthy hands. She merely pointed out that her feet were much worse!

Over the weeks, the household's dirty linen collected into a gigantic pile, and once a month all the women servants would get together for several days to do the washing. They boiled gallons of water, rubbed and beat the clothes until their arms ached, emptied buckets, pegged linen out on the line from morning till night and finally ironed everything smooth again. Professional washer-women were employed to help. They travelled from house to house and sometimes were not to be trusted. A cautious mistress used a washing tally to check how many sheets, pillowcases and other items she had sent in to wash, making sure that the same number came out again and that none had been stolen.

Food and drink

Foreign visitors to Britain in the eighteenth century were always delighted and surprised to be given slices of toast for breakfast. This meal, eaten at ten o'clock in the morning, often consisted of tea, home-made cheese, pressed tongue, and bread cut 'as thin as poppy leaves' which was sometimes toasted on a fork in front of the fire. One visitor decided it must be because English houses were so cold it was the only way to get the butter to spread!

Dinner was the main meal of the day and was usually served between two and three o'clock in the afternoon. It was an enormous meal of several dishes, such as poached salmon with fennel or caper sauce, roast beef, roast lamb, pigeon pie, and jugged hare. This was followed by plum pudding and apple tart, and the meal ended with fresh fruit. The meat was roasted on a spit over an open fire in the kitchen, whilst the pies were baked in a

brick oven. As water supplies were not very pure, homebrewed beer was drunk, with wine provided on special occasions. If there were guests, the ladies would retire to the drawing room after dinner to take tea, leaving the men round the table drinking port. They chatted for an hour or so about politics or other subjects unfit for a lady's ears, and often got rather drunk. The English dinner amazed many continental travellers, who were appalled by such gluttony. Certainly many people suffered for their over-eating and had to drink mixtures to try and cure their daily indigestion.

The last meal of the day was supper, which was generally cold meats left over from dinner. This was taken at nine o'clock in the evening, but very wealthy people usually had it much later – often after a party or a dance. It is recorded that one cook complained to his master that, although he liked his work, preparing supper at three o'clock in the morning would be the death of him!

Games and pastimes

After dark, in rooms lit only by flickering candles, the family had to make its own entertainment. Sometimes there would be a musical recital, perhaps on a viola, harpsichord, or piano. More often, games of cards, dice or dominoes were played. When there were guests, gambling on games like Hazard or Whist was often proposed to add a thrill of excitement to the evening. The bets were laid and play went on far into the night whilst winnings piled up or dwindled at an amazing rate. Occasionally someone lost so much money that, in desperation, he offered a piece of land, or even his wife or daughter, in payment of the debt – one or two eighteenth-century marriages were actually arranged in this way!

In Georgian times people gambled on everything – card games, horse races, fights, pudding-eating contests – even cricket. Many times after a quiet, leisurely game of cricket, the spectators, who had put money on the result, would suddenly leap to their feet and punch and pummel each other, shouting and arguing over the score. There were so many disputes about decisions on matches that it soon became obvious that fixed rules would have to be introduced.

In 1744 strict rules of cricket were decided. There were only two stumps and all bowling was underarm, the ball being rolled along the ground. But there were no rules about the size or the shape of the bat, and sometimes very long curved bats appeared, looking rather like hockey sticks. Each country estate had its own team and regularly challenged the neighbours to a day's cricket. Everyone joined in – the gardener playing along with the squire. The score was kept by cutting notches on a stick, and the result was counted in 'notches' rather than 'runs'. If bets had been placed, it was not uncommon to find afterwards that the scorer or a player had been bribed to influence the result of the match.

Designing a landowner's estate

Wealthy Georgian landowners wanted their grand houses to be surrounded by beautiful countryside with magnificent views in all directions. Many of these rich men employed skilled landscape gardeners who were quite ruthless about altering the grounds to make them look as 'natural' as possible. Streams were dammed to form lakes; rivers diverted to different places; trees planted or uprooted; hills levelled or created; and sometimes whole villages were demolished and rebuilt so as to be out of sight of the 'big house'.

Not content with changing what already existed, their plans became even more extravagant. Tiny classical temples were built on the tops of hills; artificial ruins placed amongst clumps of trees; elegant bridges spanned nothing but green grass and many other 'follies' appeared so that the view from the house would be interesting and special. But there remained a problem. As landowners did not want hedges or fences criss-crossing the parkland, cattle could wander freely up to the house, trampling and fouling the smooth lawns and eating the carefully tended flowers. The answer was the 'Ha-Ha', or sunken wall, named because of the exclamation of surprise when people came upon it unexpectedly. This barrier could not be seen from the windows of the house but was too steep for the animals to clamber over.

Three well-known landscape gardeners were William Kent, Sir William Chambers and Humphry Repton, but the most famous of all was Lancelot Brown. Wherever he went he would look at the ground to be landscaped, and after a moment's thought would say 'Yes, this has great capability of improvement', meaning that he could see how to make the grounds more attractive. He was very soon nicknamed 'Capability Brown'. But the amazing thing is that because trees take so long to grow, the people who actually commissioned these beautiful landscapes never saw the final effect. Though many probably didn't realize it at the time, in reality they were designing the estate for their descendants.

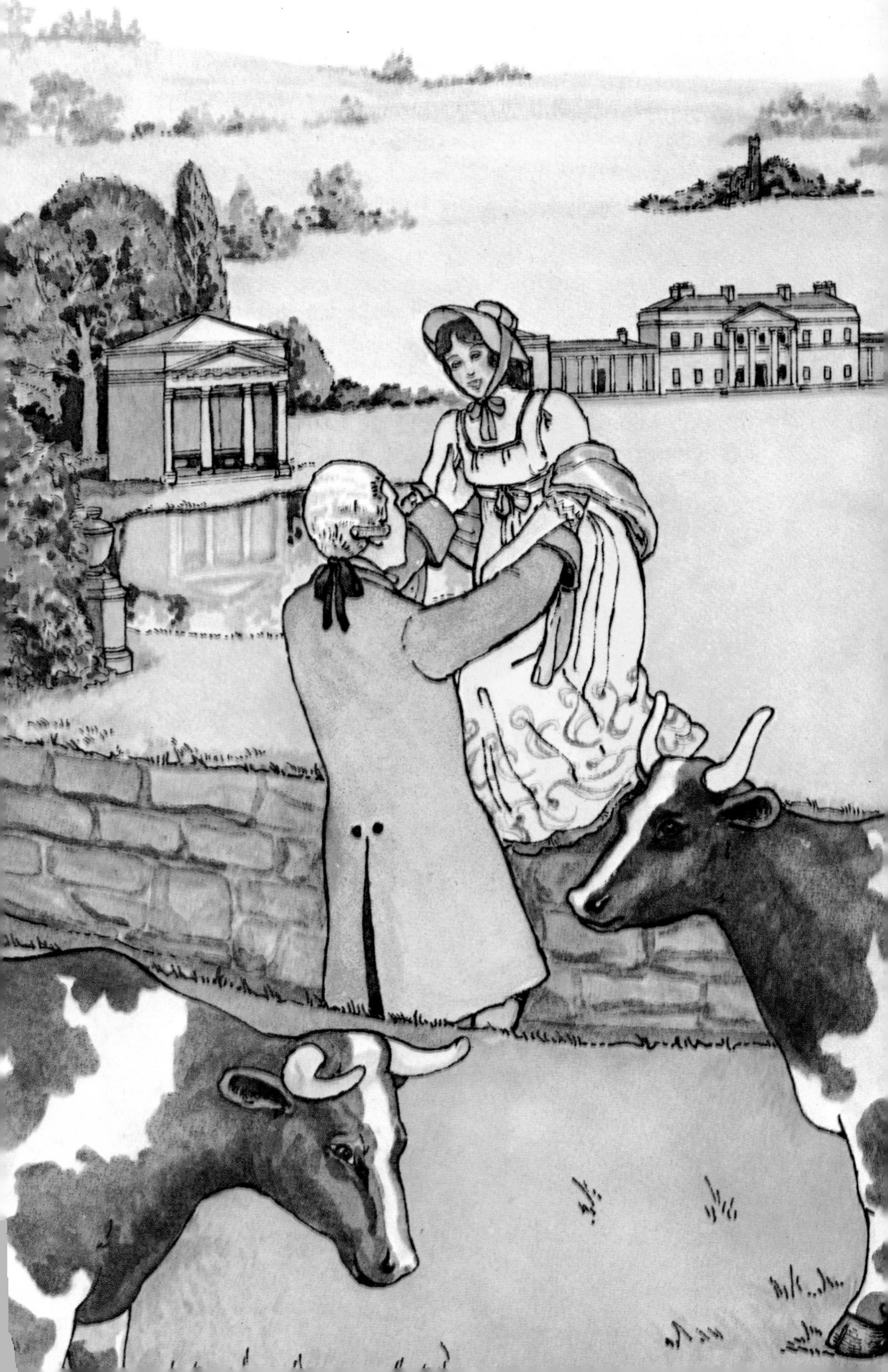

Country sports

The new interest in agriculture meant that many landowners were spending far more time on their estates instead of staying mostly in the city. As men experimented and profitable methods were introduced, farming became a rewarding and fascinating occupation.

But apart from planning their crops and creating beautiful estates for themselves, the country gentry found other joys in the countryside. Since so many trees in the forests had been felled for timber, there were fewer places for deer to live. Gradually their numbers were declining and fox hunting began to replace deer hunting as a sporting pastime. The red fox, streaking between cover across the open countryside, was an exciting animal to chase on horseback. The huntsmen, blowing their horns and yelling encouragement, eagerly followed the hounds, leaping hedgerows and splashing through streams. It was an exhilarating and challenging sport and became increasingly popular as more and more fields were enclosed and drained.

Horses were carefully bred for their strength, stamina and speed. Many country gentlemen owned racehorses, as well as hunters, and eagerly entered them at race meetings hoping to win the valuable prize money. But it was not only the wealthy who enjoyed a day at the races. Anyone, whether he owned a horse or not, could bet a few pennies, or a few guineas, on his favourite, convinced that he would go home a richer man. Unfortunately, so many terrible brawls broke out at the finish of each race, that in 1751 the Jockey Club was formed to establish some control. They introduced a very firm discipline into flat racing and insisted that there was no appeal against the Steward's decision.

Before the invention of the flintlock gun, it had been a matter of tremendous good luck, rather than skill, to hit a bird in flight. But when the shotgun was invented people found it much easier to hit game in mid-air. During the reign of George I, landowners began to take this sport seriously and the king himself is said to have shot both a pheasant and a partridge in flight at Windsor Forest in 1717.

So with hunting the fox, shooting game in the woods and fields, catching fish from the ponds and streams, and attending race meetings, life in the country was full of sporting interests – providing a variety of meats and many energetic ways to entertain visitors.

Children and their new toys

A new attitude to children was emerging. They were no longer expected to be serious all the time and behave like miniature adults. At last they were allowed to play and enjoy themselves. Children's books, which had been solemn and dull, were now written and illustrated to amuse as well as educate. 'A Little Pretty Pocket Book' by John Newbery, published in 1744, was one of the first of these to appear and became an immediate success. He soon published many more books which used exciting tales and colourful pictures to teach children the difference between right and wrong, and good and bad.

Wealthy parents began to buy toys for their children. Jigsaw puzzles, called 'dissected puzzles', were used to teach geography, history and even morals. One puzzle showed a tree with the fruits of stealing, lying and gambling hanging from bare twisted branches, and the fruits of kindness, bravery and sobriety blossoming on strong, leafy branches. These puzzles, made in mahogany, and hand cut, were very expensive.

Paper cut-outs, wooden dolls with glass eyes, china tea sets, rocking horses, model ships, and, later, metal soldiers and animals were some of the mass-produced toys that could be bought in the new toy shops opening in the cities. But on country estates, local carpenters often made individual 'baby houses' – beautiful, tiny replicas of grand houses with delicate furniture to match. They also made detailed models of farm wagons to trundle across the nursery floor. Noah's Arks, handcarved by French prisoners-of-war from tiny scraps of wood, were eagerly bought by rich parents – a strange benefit from the Napoleonic Wars!

School

Education for girls was regarded as unimportant because people thought that too much knowledge would make them unfeminine. The daughters of rich men were not sent to school but had governesses at home who taught them useful skills like reading, writing, household accounts, needlework and cooking, with perhaps a little French or Italian. Usually they learnt to play a musical instrument. This was often the pianoforte, which had been invented in Italy in 1709 and which gradually replaced the clavichord and harpsichord.

Many upper-class boys had tutors at home, but some attended grammar or public schools. Because the roads were so muddy and pot-holed it was often easier for a boy to stay at a boarding school rather than travel a few miles daily to the local school. Fashionable 'public' schools like Eton, Harrow, Westminster, Winchester and Rugby took more and more fee-paying pupils. Boys were taught

mainly Latin and Greek – other subjects were paid for as 'extras' and there were no organized games. Younger boys had to 'fag' for older boys, fetching and carrying, making their beds and often being beaten and bullied for no good reason. The masters had very little control, and during this period schools were often in a state of uproar; sometimes actual riots broke out. At Rugby the boys mined the headmaster's study with gunpowder and burned all their desks on a huge bonfire. A squad of soldiers was quickly summoned to crush this rebellion.

When they left school, young men went to university at Oxford or Cambridge where they 'discussed' the classics, or went on a Grand Tour with a tutor. For one or two years they journeyed about France and Italy, learning languages, polishing their manners and studying Art. On these Grand Tours was founded much of the interest in Italian and French painting, architecture and sculpture that dominated the English eighteenth century.

Clothes

Young men who had been on the Grand Tour of Europe brought back the most amazing new ideas of fashion. Some of them paraded around wearing huge wigs made with great folds of powdered hair, richly embroidered waistcoats and delicate tight-fitting shoes. They were immediately ridiculed. Nonetheless many people could not resist copying them. Women's hair styles in particular became increasingly complicated. Their own hair, with false padding, was swept upwards over a wire frame and elaborately decorated with garlands of flowers, bunches of artificial grapes and even stuffed birds precariously perched amongst the ringlets. Because these creations took so long to prepare, they were not taken down at night, and made wonderfully cosy places for lice and vermin to live in. People became used to seeing an occasional mouse darting in and out of a woman's curls. Cartoons often ridiculed this fashion; one showed men desperately trying to put out the blaze in a lady's hair. She had piled it so tall that it had caught alight from the candles on the chandelier!

In the country fashions were never so extreme, but gradually new styles were adopted, often influenced by the clothes worn in London. Men dressed in heavy coats, long waistcoats, knee breeches and white stockings. Women wore rich brocade dresses with tightly laced bodices over hooped petticoats. Sometimes their skirts were so enormous it was impossible for two ladies to pass each other on the stairs! Many men shaved their heads and wore wigs, changing into a cloth turban or nightcap for evenings at home. When natural hair became fashionable again, it was thickly powdered in white, blue or red, until a tax on powder in 1795 made it very expensive and therefore unpopular.

Over the years clothes became more natural and less brilliantly coloured too. Women began wearing lighter, softer fabrics, low-heeled shoes and flowing, high-waisted dresses influenced by the French Empire line popular in France after the Revolution. Men's clothes became much more sober and the fine velvet and embroidered jackets and waistcoats were replaced by plainer materials and simpler, more comfortable styles.

At the beginning of the century both boys and girls wore dresses with pretty petticoats until they were four or five years old. Then the boys were 'breeched' and had to wear the same style of clothes as their fathers. Girls continued to wear dresses with long, full skirts which made it very difficult for them to run about and play games. It was not long before children were given more freedom. Trousers instead of breeches were introduced for boys, and girls' skirts were made shorter, but they had to wear long frilly pantaloons so that they did not show their legs!

Travel and holidays

Although improved methods of road-building were slowly being introduced, transporting the growing numbers of people and goods from the country to the towns was incredibly difficult. Heavy coaches and wagons made deep ruts in the thick mud with their narrow wheels, and vehicles often capsized, flinging their passengers into dirty puddles or even over hedges! Wheels broke on the rutted roads and many horses stumbled or went lame. Highwaymen, eager for the valuable pickings of money and jewelry, were a common hazard. Nevertheless, the prospect of the appalling journeys did nothing to dampen the new enthusiasm for going up to town for a few weeks, or to the seaside for a holiday.

Because so little was known about medicine and people ate such vast quantities of rich food there was an almost frantic interest in anything that would cure illness or ease indigestion. The City of Bath was famed for its health-giving springs and many people travelled there every year to stay and take the waters. Each morning they sat in the warm baths for an hour or so. After breakfast it was time for a visit to the Pump Room. Here they sipped the cloudy, mineral-filled water. Three glasses a day were recommended and there were very mixed opinions about its taste! The Pump Room soon became the fashionable centre of Bath where everyone of importance met and, having taken the waters, planned the busy social round for the rest of the day.

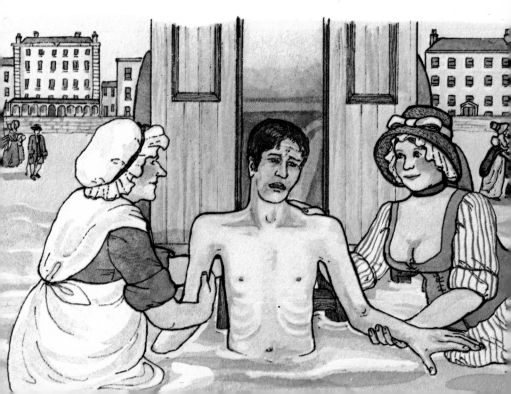

The success of spa towns like Bath, Harrogate and Tunbridge Wells, with their warm springs and hundreds of fashionable visitors, led people to investigate the possibilities of cold-water bathing. Dr Richard Russell wrote a book about the health-giving properties of salt water, and soon seaside resorts such as Brighton, Margate and Scarborough began to thrive as popular places for the aristocracy and gentry to spend their holidays. Modesty forbade people to be only partially clothed on the beach, so Benjamin Beale invented bathing machines. Horses dragged these small wheeled huts a discreet distance into the sea, where the braver bathers could leap into the water and splash around. More timid ones ventured reluctantly down the ladder to be ducked by women known as 'dippers'.

In the winter, when there was not much to be done on the estate, the master rented a house in London and the whole family went to the City for the Season. Here they spent an exciting and exhausting month or two seeing the sights, visiting each other to effect introductions between marriageable daughters and eligible young men, attending all the important balls, and going to see the latest plays at the theatre. Foreigners were astonished at the rowdy audiences, especially the crowd in the gallery who, as one German visitor remarked, made far more noise for one shilling each than he did for his three shillings in the pit!

At the end of the Season the families returned once more to their estates to plant and reap their crops, tend their livestock and plan and build for the future.

Some of the Georgian Houses owned by The National Trust

Antony House, Torpoint, Cornwall
Attingham Park, Atcham, Shrewsbury, Salop
Basildon Park, Pangbourne, Berkshire
Beningbrough Hall, Shipton-by-Beningbrough, Shipton, N.
Yorkshire
Berrington Hall, Leominster, Herefordshire
Buscot, Lechlade, Oxfordshire
Castle Coole, Enniskillen, Co Fermanagh, N. Ireland
Castle Ward, Strangford, Downpatrick, Co Down, N. Ireland
Clandon Park, West Clandon, Guildford, Surrey
Erddig, Wrexham, Clwyd
Farnborough Hall, Warmington, Banbury, Oxfordshire
Florence Court, Enniskillen, Co Fermanagh, N. Ireland
Ickworth, Horringer, Bury St Edmunds, Suffolk
Nostell Priory, Wakefield, W. Yorkshire
Ormesby Hall, Ormesby, Middlesbrough, Cleveland
Osterley Park, Isleworth, Middlesex
Peckover House, Wisbech, Cambridgeshire
Philipps House, Dinton Park, Salisbury, Wiltshire
Plas Newydd, Llanfairpwll, Isle of Anglesey, Gwynedd
Shugborough, Stafford, Staffordshire
Stourhead House, Stourton, Warminster, Wiltshire
Tatton Park, Knutsford, Cheshire
Uppark, South Harting, Petersfield, West Sussex
Upton House, Banbury, Oxfordshire
West Wycombe Park, West Wycombe, Buckinghamshire
Wimpole Hall, Cambridge, Cambridgeshire